better together*

*This book is best read together, grownup and kid.

 akidsco.com

a
kids
book
about

a
kids
book
about
Unconscious
Bias

by Wendy Batchelder

A Kids Co.
Editors Jennifer Goldstein and Emma Wolf
Designer Jelani Memory
Creative Director Rick DeLucco
Studio Manager Kenya Feldes
Sales Director Melanie Wilkins
Head of Books Jennifer Goldstein
CEO and Founder Jelani Memory

DK
Delhi Technical Team Bimlesh Tiwary Pushpak Tyagi, Rakesh Kumar
Senior Production Editor Jennifer Murray
Senior Production Controller Louise Minihane
Senior Acquisitions Editor Katy Flint
Acquisitions Project Editor Sara Forster
Managing Art Editor Vicky Short
Managing Director, Licensing Mark Searle

First American edition, 2025
Published in the United States by DK Publishing, 1745 Broadway, 20th Floor,
New York, NY 10019

First published in Great Britain in 2025 by
Dorling Kindersley Limited, 20 Vauxhall Bridge Road, London SW1V 2SA
A Penguin Random House Company

The authorised representative in the EEA is
Dorling Kindersley Verlag GmbH. Arnulfstr. 124, 80636 Munich, Germany

A catalog record for this book is available from the Library of Congress.
A CIP catalogue record for this book is available from the British Library.
ISBN: 978-0-2417-4379-9

DK books are available at special discounts when purchased in bulk for sales
promotions, premiums, fund-raising, or education use. For details, contact:
DK Publishing Special Markets, 1745 Broadway, 20th Floor, New York, NY 10019
SpecialSales@dk.com

Printed and bound in China
www.dk.com
akidsco.com

MIX
Paper | Supporting
responsible forestry
FSC™ C018179

This book was made with Forest
Stewardship Council™ certified
paper – one small step in DK's
commitment to a sustainable future.
Learn more at www.dk.com/uk/
information/sustainability

I dedicate this to my 6 kids and to all kids who have ever felt misunderstood, judged, unwelcome, different.

May you find beauty in differences and understand others more as a result of exploring your own unconscious bias.

Intro
for grownups

Bias can be a tough subject to tackle, because it happens so often. Our brains are predisposed to try to make sense of the world—to classify, to understand. To explore bias means to explore our assumptions, our own experiences, and to challenge the way we think.

We all have biases.

The challenge becomes: do we want to do something about it?

This book is designed to provide a call to action: explore your own bias and challenge the bias of other people, as you see it. Challenge from a place of curiosity, of exploration, not judgment. Ultimately, seek to understand versus to be understood.

Have you ever felt misunderstood without even saying a word?

Have you ever felt like someone thought they understood *who you are* before they knew anything about you?

Have you ever felt that who you are is **less important** than who people think you are?

That i

s bias.

Bias is when someone assumes something about you

without knowing you.

Bias can happen because of what someone looks like, where they were born, or what they wear.

And this bias can be

conscious or unconscious.

Conscious bias is when you have assumptions about a person and you know you're making those assumptions—the bias is intentional, and you know you are doing it.

(And in case you don't know, an assumption is when you think something is true, but you don't have all the facts. You could be wrong.)

Unconscious bias is when you have assumptions about a person and you don't even know you have that bias—it's unintentional, and you don't know you are doing it.

When I was a kid, a lot of people assumed that because I was adopted, I was not wanted.

That wasn't true.

What *was* true is that I was wanted
by both my biological parents
and my adoptive parents.

This **unconscious bias** really hurt me.

Sometimes it still does, and I'm a grownup now.

Understanding
unconscious bias
and knowing

we all
have it

is important,
and that's why
we're here!

By examining our bias, we have the opportunity to move unconscious bias to our conscious mind, and then we can do something about it.

We can work on this together.

So, how do we dig in?

It sta
with
 cur

When we start thinking about our thoughts, we can understand our bias better.

Why do we think certain things about others?

Where did these thoughts come from?

What can we do about it?

Well, in my example, here's what I learned and did.

First, I felt really bad because of what other people said about me, and I let their assumptions become my truth.

I listened to the things people said about me instead of correcting their assumptions.

If I was there again, now, I'd ask:

Why do you think that about me?
Do you know why kids are adopted?

I would challenge their assumptions.

And then, I could begin to share the facts.

Learning new information
can work to eradicate bias.

Facts

are
facts–

they remain unchanged.

However, my feelings and their feelings about families could change.

And the funny thing is, I assumed that all biological families were wanted, accepted by default, and felt like they belonged more than I did.

And that isn't *always* the case.

Facts
consi

are
stent.

Feelings are *not* consistent.

It's helpful to focus on
what we can change...

instead of what we can't.

Feelings exist in the past, present, and future.

How did I **feel** about it then?

How do I **feel** about it now?

How might I **feel** about it in the future?

Think about a time when you made an assumption about someone.

These are examples of bias:

Women love to cook.

Men love to drive cars.

A tall person must be
good at basketball.

A person with glasses
loves to read.

A person who wears dresses
must not like soccer.

Someone of Indian descent
must have been born in India.

What else might be true?

All genders can enjoy cooking.

Women can love cars.

A tall person can be interested in any sport, like gymnastics.

A person with glasses may prefer to learn by listening.

Someone of Indian descent may be from Chicago.

You get it, right?

By being curious about our thoughts, we can bring the unconscious thoughts to the surface, make them conscious, and learn more about ourselves and others.

Doing this gives us the opportunity to make a choice. Do we continue to believe our assumptions, or do we seek to understand and challenge our assumptions based on new knowledge?

This practice gives us the opportunity to **truly connect** with people, and that's an **AMAZING** thing.

When you catch yourself or others making assumptions about someone, consider asking what else could be true.

ST
CURI

AY
OUS!

Bring the unconscious to the conscious, and be **open to learning** something you didn't know before.

This **brings us together** instead of separating us further from one another.

Imagine how cool that would be!

Who knows, you might **make a new friend.**

Outro
for grownups

Bias is something we need to continue to explore, so don't let the work end here. Today is just the beginning!

Continue to ask yourself and your kids:

Why do I think that?

What else might be true?

Can I learn something new?

We can continue to explore our own thoughts and those of other people to learn more about what bias is, move our subconscious thoughts to consciousness, and work to make the world a more inclusive place, for everyone!

About The Author

Wendy Batchelder (she/her) is a 2-time Chief Data Officer in the technology industry with a broad understanding of how to take highly technical aspects of data management and translate them into simple, concise, business-valued solutions that are practical and simple to understand.

Her background has led her to lead global data & analytics organizations at 3 Fortune 500 companies. She approaches situations with curiosity and humility, which has led to creating innovative data solutions for complex challenges to deliver measurable value.

A lifelong learner, Wendy graduated from Miami University with a B.S. in Accounting and Information Systems, from Drake University with a Masters of Accountancy, from University of Iowa with an Executive MBA, and pursues ongoing education through Harvard Business School. Her work history includes EY, KPMG, Aviva, Wells Fargo, VMware, and Salesforce.

Wendy resides in West Des Moines, Iowa, with her husband and their 6 kids.

 @wendybatchelder   wendybatchelder.com

Made to empower.

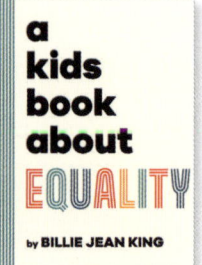

Discover more at akidsco.com